# WATCH OUT

*Selected Poems of Kuno Raeber*

# WATCH OUT

*Selected Poems of* Kuno Raeber

*Translated from the German by* Stuart Friebert

LOST HORSE PRESS
Sandpoint, Idaho

# ACKNOWLEDGEMENTS

This volume would not be possible without the support of Friederike Barakat, and the permission of Carl Hanser Verlag, Munich to publish these poems. Additional thanks to Christiane Wyrwa for a number of helpful suggestions.

Great thanks to the editors of the following journals, who published some of the poems:

> *Field*
> *New Delta Review*
> *Pleiades*
> *Prairie Schooner*
> *Rattle*
> *Solstice*
> *World Literature Today*

The cover photograph of Kuno Raeber courtesy of scaneg Verlag München (Joerg Trobitius).
*Stuart Friebert's Photograph by* Cindy Sanders.
*Christiane Wyrwa's Photograph by* Gustav Drechsler, scaneg Verlag Munich.
*Book & Cover Design:* Christine Holbert.

FIRST EDITION

This and other fine LOST HORSE PRESS titles may be viewed online at www.losthorsepress.org.

LIBRARY OF CONGRESS CATALOGING-IN-PUBLICATION DATA

Names: Raeber, Kuno, 1922-1992, author. | Friebert, Stuart, 1963- translator.
Title: Selected poems of Kuno Raeber / translated from the German by Stuart Friebert.
Description: First edition. | Sandpoint, Idaho : Lost Horse Press, 2016.
Identifiers: LCCN 2016028099 | ISBN 9780996858427 (trade paper : alk. paper)
Subjects: LCSH: Raeber, Kuno, 1922-1992.—Translations into English.
Classification: LCC PT2678.A265 .A2 2016 | DDC 831/.914—dc23
LC record available at https://lccn.loc.gov/2016028099

*In Memory of Kuno Raeber*
*& my great teacher, Werner Vordtriede*

# TABLE OF CONTENTS

## III   *Steps, Winding*

# IV   *And Always Go On*

THE SWISS POET Kuno Raeber (1922 – 1992) grew up in Lucerne, the center of Catholic Switzerland. Looking back at his school days he said, "For me the church contained everything, there was no reality outside the church." In January 1945, he felt so tormented by religious troubles that he entered the Jesuit novitiate in order to overcome his doubts. After a few months the experiment ended in disaster. He ran away and sank into "an ice cave of depression."

Two years later, travelling to Rome, Raeber said it was the light of the Mediterranean that began seeding a spiritual rebirth in his despair. The Catholic world of his past, in his words "the father- and mother-house full of beloved images, consolations, and dreams," no longer seemed to be lost forever, but in the welcome new light of the South the beliefs and images appeared to be part of a much broader tradition that also comprised the mythical heritage of Greek and Roman civilization.

This experience proved to be the starting point of his lifelong effort to build a poetic cosmos that replaced the lost world of the church, its mythology, and its order. He said, "As in my youth the church contained everything, today the world of art—the world of the words that I produce, contains everything."

"This historical sense of the timeless as well as of the temporal and of the timeless and the temporal together, is what makes a writer traditional," T.S. Eliot, whom Raeber had newly discovered around 1950, wrote in *Tradition and the Individual Talent*. Raeber wanted to be a traditional writer, but in 1952, when he went to live in Germany, that was not an easy thing to do. Raeber worked as a lecturer in history at the universities of Tübingen and Hamburg, and the young people he met there were ex-Nazi-soldiers, who had been POWs and become conscious of the crimes and atrocities of the past years. As Hans Magnus Enzensberger wrote, "After the entry of the Allies, Germany was mute, in the most precise meaning of the word, a speechless country."

But in Raeber's diary of 1953 we read that "Today people are obsessed with the idea that we must invent a new language in order to say something entirely new. But our aim must be to write the most simple, authentic, and pure language, we must continue going the way which the great poets of our language have shown us." For a Swiss, the great tradition in writing poetry had remained unbroken, and although Raeber speaks of "our" language, for many of his German contemporaries he seemed to come from a strange background, not from a country close by.

During his first years in Germany Raeber could publish only a few poems in literary magazines, but before he completed the volume, *The Transformed Ships* (*Die verwandelten Schiffe*), he had filled hundreds of pages in his diaries with thoughts on poetry, as well as several notebooks with first drafts of poems. The book was published in 1957, preceded by brief remarks Raeber called "The Poem Today." The essence of his ideas about poetry, they remained virtually unchanged for the rest of life.

In Raeber's view, we live in a time of syncretism, and all periods of cultural history are made simultaneously accessible by poetry, which can make us see their correspondences and transformations. As the words of poetry cannot create a 'true image' of the world, they perform a masquerade showing splinters and reflections in layers and stratifications, which he later called "palimpsest."

"For me, poetry is a masquerade where there is no unmasking but only the trying-on of ever new masks," he wrote. But the masks are not instruments of deception, they use opposites and contraries which move toward balance and harmony. Raeber repeats these convictions in many essays, stressing that poetry is an invocation of images that strive to come closer and closer to the "true image" which can never be attained. The invocation or incantation of the poetic process calls for a system of repetitions and variations that binds words and sound together. Repetitive images and sounds also constitute the structure and patterns in his prose works, so that the principles he employs in the poems pervade his entire body of work. After his youthful attempts, Raeber never used rhymes or definite meters again. He said writing his verse in lines should guide the reader in experiencing the right rhythm. He'd read every poem very slowly with a strong emphasis on all movements. After pausing a few seconds, he'd say "And now I'm going to read it again" — then follow with a quicker reading to stress the rhythmic unity.

Poetry was the highest spiritual achievement for Raeber, who considered the poet the legitimate successor of the priests, prophets, and magicians of religious eras. Once we accept that the realms of dreams, fantasy, myth, and legend are as real for him as the normal everyday world, his poems are not difficult to understand. And that is exactly what the selection in *Watch Out* helps us do, by presenting a great variety of forms and topics, and asking us to join in Raeber's swift transformations from the past to the present, from the real to the magical, by the power of his words.

The first section opens with "Words," the shortest of all his poems, but it encompasses the poet's whole world. It is followed by "The Rose" and several of Raeber's opposites and contraries like "Turned Away Turned Toward" or "Down and Up." Of these "Inside and Outside" shows a subtle playing with a very old image: ever since the early Greeks' fluttering breezes in groves signaled the presence of the gods. In Thomas Mann's "Doctor Faustus," for instance, his ring is engraved with a line on the fluttering breeze in the grove, symbolizing the divine aura of the artist. But here the poet must "devour everything and gulp everything down," because his poetry doesn't describe the world outside but comes from "the images inside."

Although most of the poems of the second section have titles like "Cloud," "Storm," or "Rain," they are not simple presentations of weather situations or aspects of external reality. "Road" for instance begins "A rose bursts open the middle of the road," and ends with a variation of these words. The poems let their various objects move from real situations into magical surroundings as in "The Motorcycle," whose sound makes an everyday vehicle glide into the primeval forest. In "Metamorphosis of the Lions" a girl lives through a whole fairy tale night after night. A lion comes into her room, and when she kisses him, the lion is changed into a prince and then immediately into a stone. In many poems an object is mentioned—rose, egg, mirror, pyramid—which has special significance in Raeber's oeuvre but is not explained, so the reader must be patient, enjoy the sound of the images in their poetic coherence and abstain from looking for rationally understandable connections.

The third section begins with poems about places. For most present-day Germans, Frankfurt means a financial center. Some will remember it as Goethe's birthplace. But in the poem, "Frankfurt," it's important as the city that witnessed the coronation of the last emperor of the Holy Roman Empire in 1764. The fact that Goethe watched the ceremony in his youth adds other associations. But the poem doesn't require detailed historical information. This is also true for "Rome" and "Escorial." These two places are closely connected by the figure of St. Lawrence, who suffered martyrdom in Rome and in whose honor the Spanish palace was erected. In Raeber's later writing, St. Lawrence appears as a configuration drifting into a central position because in him the laurel of Apollo—God of poetry in the Greek tradition—is combined with the patron saint of Rome with the laurel in his name, so that the figure appears as a complex symbol. The saint is never mentioned; only attributes call his hidden energy into presence, such as the gridiron and the coals, bones, and the smell of burnt flesh. Another mixture of reality and magic is the city of "New York": "always built higher collap- / sing and torn / down and tirelessly / begun again between both / rivers of Paradise con- / cocted of a thousand / sounds." Seeing New York was a deeply moving experience for Raeber, and he compared the effects on his life and his writing only to the experience of seeing Rome. Even if the reader can't catch all the implications, these poems with their numbered parts and stanzas of different length should be read together, so that the forward or backward or circling movements of the entire composition can be followed.

In the last section the opening poem, "Listening," presents a special form. It consists of six repetitions of the word "listening," one at the beginning, three in the middle, and two at the end; in between there are only words taken from the first strophe of Hölderlin's elegy "Bread and Wine." But in the poem the two voices are blended and united in a close sequence of beautiful sounds. In "Halcyon Days," Raeber brings an old tale from Ovid's *Metamorphoses* into the life of the poet who is "chewing / the bitter leaf soft," sitting on the cliff where the storms "drag / the kingfisher's mate into the foam." The last selection ends with a poem that appropriately begins, "And in the end / the walls give way on both / sides."

The translator Stuart Friebert has selected and arranged the poems in *Watch Out* so that they present various aspects of Kuno Raeber's writing, and he is highly qualified for this task. In 1965, he wrote his first letter to Raeber asking permission to print four poems in an anthology of contemporary German poetry. Two of the poems mentioned in that letter, "Metamorphosis of the Lions" and "Cardinal," appear in *Watch Out*. Friebert not only visited Raeber in Europe, inviting him to read to a group of students, he also proposed that Raeber come to Oberlin College for a year while Friebert took a sabbatical in Zürich. Raeber agreed, becoming the first Max Kade Writer-in-Residence, initiating a program that continues to this day.

When Raeber returned to Europe, he encouraged Friebert to keep translating his poems, many of which subsequently appeared in the journals, more recently in a first collection, *Be Quiet,* to which *Watch Out* is a companion volume. Thus the translator has been practicing close readings of these poems for half a century, and his versions match Raeber's vocabulary as well as exhibit a special skill in the exact reproduction of the rhythmic patterns that constitute the lines of the poems.

All in all, *Watch Out* presents the reader with the really essential aspects of the poetic achievement of Kuno Raeber. What remains to say is: Take up and read!

—*Christiane Wyrwa*

# The Quiet Quaking I

Words are residue. Afterward
neither trees nor houses. The glacier
glossy in the silence.

Window wings. Numbed
butterflies. The wind.
The awakening.
Watch out.

Snatch everything for yourself and devour
everything and gulp
everything down. No fluttering
in the grove anymore. Inside
the grove and inside
the fluttering. And outside
nothing more.

## THE GLASS HOUSE

The angels open
his glass house daily all right, but only
to lift him quickly into
the air till the treetop
whips him and he fears
he'll plunge down into the puddle of oil by the garage.

People blowing horns and shouting
don't hear the quarrel
neighboring angels are stirring up with his angels,
who travel furiously back and forth, tugging away
and let him really fall, almost.

But safely back again in the glass house, he smashes,
raising a hand in order to greet
someone passing by, the wall
and throws the broken bits
right into his face,
so that he wipes the blood
from his forehead with his handkerchief and runs off.

His angels go silent; but
they'll pay back the burden of
cutting a new pane, cementing it,
when they take wing tomorrow.

The rose the thorn
of the rose the prick
of the thorn of the rose the blood
from the prick of the thorn of the rose
red and red
the leaves of the rose the rose.

Under the glow
raging roses.
The wind.
Shadows only in the white
tents. In the tents
the stillness.

In the garden only the
roaring breath of the sea.
The silver of the deep and the
millennia golden
melted in the ether.
But on your hand the black
beetle
listless with feelers.

Elevated and
laden with trappings with
trinkets and stones
above the desert.
And then the dunes and only
just a little rise too. The butterfly
tiny and white in the gardens
beyond the quicksand.

## AND ALTOGETHER

And altogether
the humming in the grass and
the beetles and the
buzzing of bumblebees and
from the airplanes just the quiet
quaking of the ground
in your ear.

Suddenly shadows.
Yet still the
warmth in the grass the bright
edge around the cloud.
And from the trees a gentle
wind without malice.

# TWILIGHT

Twilight and a gentle breeze
from the meadows.
The path
a snake alone
into the unknown and white.

Motionless trees
mirrored in the pond
motionless. Always a warm
afternoon in October.
Temptation of death.

The dry
leaves feathers
rumpled and
iridescent the vacant
eyes but noon
defiant with its hundred
flashing oars
won't fall back
from the spot.

And the glint far
below so far how
could it light up the swaths
above and inside
calm in the middle
the furious torsion?

Turned away from the
houses the
dusty trees
the square with the
sharp stones
turned away from the
sheets hanging down from
the ropes the sweat of
nights in them the
fear of death and the
moaning when morning
comes on
its face turned
toward the cliffs the
reefs into the sea
in the cracks
few blossoms
but blue but red
the portal before the flood
bolted right away again
turned toward the
beach with its stones the empty
graves in the precipice
the wing gliding on without
a sound and everything
covering up the shimmer
extinguishing the
leaden ledge
the fragrance of
petrified flowers

back and forth
going astray above
turned away from the
houses the
dust and the roads
turned toward the open
portal under the over-
hanging cliff
expectation.

Submerged in the tub.
Emerged on the beach by the huts.
For years the
beating of waves.
Submerged on the beach by the huts.
Emerged in the tub.
Still the same bird
on the sill as before
agitated pecking.

And our memories black
down to all the buried
others. But our light
light-minded wishes
white
up at them instead.
And then above only
some tittering still.

# II

*Far from Dream*

Drunk, by early light, I force myself
into the garden, which stares at me through
a thousand eyes. Only
the tortoises stir, gathered together in
the wet grass, and talk over
the sights of the night.
If I were clear minded, they'd take me
into their confidence. I tumble
by to the last
window lit up, as if I could save it
from dying. Someone's
already sharpened tomorrow's
sun-dagger behind the horizon.

# CLOUD

Only a cloud. But without
the glimmer of lambs grazing
on our side the moon
cracked and colorless.

Bent over, the chickens pick
the seeds out of the hoarfrost and don't
look back at the high terrace, where
from the railing the feathers of the dead
turkey swing. They do not look
down to the lower terrace, where the ostrich
stalks and amid cries
breaks into the ice,
which mirrors it brazenfaced.

It's still standing, still hanging, the heavy
egg over the flat roof
where they're sunning themselves. But
the egg will break into pieces, the water
splash down on the flat roof. They'll
pack their jackets and take off.
The egg will travel, pour
its water down into the streets
and only stop again over the arid
gardens, to fill
the ponds. Soon it'll stand,
soon it'll hang, the light
egg over the gardens and close.

A rose bursts open the middle of the road,
the bumblebee
awakens and shoots
into the pane, falls back on the sill.
Thorns
block the road, and the rose catches,
hidden and greedy,
cars, flies in its mesh.
Out over the stunned bumblebee wafts
the fragrance of a rose, which
bursts the middle of the road open.

We're always on the steep descent toward summer.
Ahead to be sure the bicyclists
in their white caps and striped
tricots whiz by. But
they don't arrive before
us down in the middle chamber of summer,
where you're in a scarlet shawl,
on the stool,
whose varnish is peeling off,
combing yourself, carefully blackening your eyelids
before the mirror, and looking at them
and all of us below at the end of the steep
descent in the middle chamber of summer,
indifferently,
indifferent pharaoh.

# THE MOTORCYCLE

The motorcycle's rusty. Its racket
is more like the racket
of bizarre birds of the jungle.
He's decomposed, and a minute before the storm
the mist breaks forth from the pavement.

The motorcycle's rusty, and who
will recognize it as soon as it
leans against a giant fern? Then only
the birds will make a racket, the jungle
feeds the next decomposition.

The motorcycle
throws him off into the puddle:
sea, sea. His jacket
sucks itself full of the sun falling
behind the rim.

Tattered
faces cast laughter at him
in the puddle. His jacket
sucks itself full of the sun falling
behind the rim.

He lies in the puddle, gurgling.
and a bubble. In the summer
the girl on the beach stepped
on a jellyfish, waited till he was there.

The motorcycle
throws him off into the puddle. The girl, tattered,
casts laughter at him, blows him a kiss. He lies
in the brown water, gurgling, a bubble:
sea, sea, and behind the rim
sun staggering.

# METAMORPHOSIS OF THE LIONS

The girl cries in the morning and drinks her milk and forgets
   the nightly lion.

But the next night, from the corner behind
the cupboard, another lion emerges
and fills up the room with his muzzle and his mane.
And the girl kisses him even though she trembles.
And as a reward the lion changes into a prince.
But princes suffer kisses no better than lions:
He freezes and lies, a block of stone, in the corner of the room.

The girl cries in the morning and drinks her milk and forgets
   the nightly lion.

But in the next night she will be sure to kiss the new lion
   once again.
Soon all the foundlings lie in all corners of the room,
left behind by the nightly glaciers.
Visitors pretend not to see anything;
they surely know nothing about the second of the prince.

The girl cries in the morning and drinks her milk and forgets
   the nightly lion.

You can't
singe the coat with your mirror
of both panthers running
down the steps vying with
each other. They run
too fast. The children
draw them into their dance-circle
and sing. The panthers
jump in great
leaps outside to the other side and eat
the fish going silent.

Upright, you'll
shoot up at some point mute and shackled
on the stony seat in back, scared
from sleep and see
the rooster, its eyes smashed
to splinters, broken in pieces on the pavement.
But like then, remember? remember?,
a single cricket will
chirp, which doesn't fear freezing to death.
And look, outside
there's someone still pushing, like then, his new
bicycle by and whistling.

The bottles stand in the entrance.
You stumble. The blind
bust doesn't smell the blood,
which is mixing with cat
urine. The broom
bursts forth from behind the fountain into the pool
and plunges into the shards and does
not get wet and does not cut itself.

## RAIN

Cowering
in the last corner,
birds, blind behind a veil spraying about.
Rain runs down and tears it to pieces,
glues seeds
to the earth. The birds,
above the wind again, cradle
themselves with dripping wings
on the wires and blink
into the distance.

The bird will not stray
in and catch fire from
the curtain. It beats
the lamps with its wings so
they wobble. Feathers fall
between the houses.
There are hiding places
under the roofs. Its blood
drips onto a white
cooler. It whirs
back and forth between the walls
and sees the marble gleam
on the pavement. It shoots
down. The children
will find it.

The winged spring and the scattered
feather-leaves lie under the black
ant-snow of their winter,
which still would melt this flat image on the ground
quickly formed by the car's fall-wheel
from the stuff and color of the pattern
if from the edge of the road
the boy, casting his visual net, hadn't
drawn it into the pool
of his eyes, which are still blinking above
his mouth, chewing an apple noisily:
far from dream and the stormy
summer, which is siphoning the image
up from the ground where it's long
been, having swung back and forth
on the surface and finally sunk
down, to be seen later once more,
clear, black and teeming.

Found lost in the moss
found under the leaves
under the foliage under the grass the withered
flowers lost in the
hole under the earth in the covered up
hidden site under
rubble and under
rocks and under
love and death and
this life and beyond
found down there
inaccessible and unreachable
and uncertain and yet more than anything
certain and steadfast and always
firm and always
whole in the center
lost found.

# III

*Steps, Winding*

Run from the center
out through the allees
run and don't stop at the
abandoned cemetery
don't walk through the narrow
gate don't climb down into
the vault of bones odor of
puddles sourish sweetish
the tissue handkerchiefs
soaked
above the traffic light
some squeaking a
car stops and
don't stop keep running
over the bridge the
middle brightly reflected in the cloudy
sky the de-
parted leaning
against the trees don't stop
don't stop and run
back over
the other bridge
through the portal without
wings no entrance
no exit back
don't stop don't stop
run
agleam into the mummy and
can't be waked
right into its midst.

*I The Eagle*

He rose up
from Vienna and over
the Black Forest appearing
as an indigenous bird and yet
it was presumably in the Persian upland where he
slipped out of the
egg but that's
too long ago over
Frankfurt he's stood
for half a millennium
from time to time again and again and some
even claim he's had
two heads for a time a mythical
animal it was said he'd been but since then
he's only been a simple
bird quite alone
for some time and without
companions and comes
across his old
nest St. Bartholomew between
the skyscrapers no longer he'd even
seemed exotic to Goethe like having
flown from a distant
tower there's a feather falling
and there a feather among passersby,
who pick it up and recall
they'd seen him recently
to the northeast sitting on a snowcapped

sandy square in the snow
emaciated and burning with
hunger billing and cooing how long
ago was it that he ate from
golden plates above the gates
of free cities and from Castel del
Monte spotted the sails of the Saracens
with the winged lion that he
dwelled comfortably in
the Palatine cavern
and still feared today
he's smarting from the smoke in his eyes
they drove him out with
yet he won't be able to keep himself
above Frankfurt anymore soon he'll
have lost all his feathers they sweep them
together at five o'clock from time
to time on Constable
Square if he's lucky he falls
down by the Römer an
emaciated carcass a Turk picks
him off the pavement and throws him with the
other garbage into the container.

## II  *The Fourteenth of July*

Not the one from 1789 in Paris
the one from 1794 in Frankfurt am Main the
fourteenth of July Goethe
was far away in Weimar Frau
Rat still was alive both
had no mind for what was
happening then when sullen

Franz of Toscana was the last to
receive the Roman crown
sacrament and invocation of a
magical order fore-
shadowing a uni-
versal Reich of eternal peace, which
still doesn't exist today and also the
League of Nations and the United
Nations are just
preliminaries less strik-
ing than the long
flight of the eagle from the Nile to the Main but
given all that more generally the crown
the holy lance were for Goethe
and for Frau Rat just
antiques the uni-
ersal was for them just a
moral understanding among humans the Reich
was a remnant
of the middle period and the crowning of the Kaiser
a cozy drama of
local history what's there
to surprise us that the
sons and grandsons forgot the Frankfurt fourteenth of July
but not Paris's and made of the
Reich a newer
panzer among the many
panzers all sealed leaded and pressing
crushing one another on the
narrow road to world
power and added to the riches the double
crown of the Upper and the
Lower Empire

there in
the zoological gardens of the museum
there's the falcon of
Horus the truly
civilized truly
rational human doesn't
understand the signs and also
lucky guy
doesn't need them anymore.

I

Rising way up the
rubble the swarms
of pigeons the dog
old her teats hanging down
the rutting
twitch of tongue the smell
still there
sharp between the stones.

II

The shadow
suddenly on the emptied
square. The grid-
iron the
dried up drops
memory of
profane of
sacred love a whir
now nearer now distant. The wheel
turning in the rain.

III *Thermal Baths of Caracalla*

The dust the
wind the
whirlpool in the portal of
the huge red
wall
and within the basins
dried up laughter

loud cheers lost in the vaults
the shit
of the birds and the embrace
later
belated in the car.

IV

And a thought
long
aloft and
not dispensed a shadow
undecided off in
that direction over the garden the roofs
seesawing and then the
gusts the abrupt
resolution of rain.

V

The stormy wind from the Palatine
coming on and then
the rain you don't need to buy
any more cake at Giolitti's just simply
jump down from the roof and
over the gusts quietly
and softly go forth
over the domes softly
and quietly forth
over the squares and when
the motorcycles down by
the Maddalena blow their
horns so loudly and when
that voice down by

the Pantheon keeps
shrieking so shrilly
o rapture
happiness of entrancement.


   VI *Thermal Baths of Caracalla 2*
And then the basin
emptied out the warm
the cold waters not even a dead
fish the attendant in a dark
suit and never bathed in the warm
never in the cold waters yet against
the rain a folded-
up newspaper.


   VII
Fragrance from flowers
never smelled the breezes
thick with clouds and
run thicker the bones
out of the bandages
and washed
away by the muddy flood.


   VIII *Catacombs*
Under the walls
you say under the roots
we should look for the entrance
into the vault:
the niches down there the walls
dripping that's more
after our hearts.

But the howling of the horns
the echo of the walls
the vault down there and of the
niches and of the walls
dripping below the roots
what do you say?

    IX  *Via Appia*
The grave
buried under
scrub the car
groans our breasts
ooze
slippery steps
the sun-shunning
plants silenced.

I

What sort of flowers what
leaves thrown away the stem
black and stamped out
the cypress
over the trees and over
pylons the
pyramid.
Or the desert crystallized
gleaming polished incantation
of death sorcer-
ess gesture against the empty
sky elevated without
solace without tears
house of cards always
more confounded always
built higher collap-
sing and torn
down and tirelessly
begun again between both
rivers of Paradise con-
cocted of a thousand
sounds. Said to be dead there
lies the hairy
giant still
just look in the grass and holds the
conch to his ear listening
and laughing.

II

Skyscrapers as new
bodies for
Venetian senators torn
down in the construction and
endlessly erected
the processions
of scarabs
of pharaohs their skin
scaly and motley
in the thicket the temple
alone in the clearing
processions
and the sacrifice on the bloody
altar blotted out
overgrown and the avenues iced over
the trees black without leaves
processions
coming from everywhere
nowhere
a grave a casting with a
weed a bone
a torn-off shred
of holy linen.


III *Sixth Avenue*

*—for Christiane Zimmer*

An Uptown wing drags
Downtown the feathers
the down plastered with tar and mud
the avenue
Uptown Downtown torn

off by the east wind the feathers
filthy the down
plastered with tar and mud
and filthy from mud the wing turquoise
no longer now
Uptown torn
off by the icy wind in last week's
snow Downtown the lovely
wing turquoise
wing no longer the feathers
heavy and filthy plastered by
tar and mud plastered
and heavy and filthy the down
glides down in the snow of last
week lying
there blackish
Uptown the avenue
Downtown turquoise
wing no more week now
plastered blackish and heavy and
filthy lying there the feathers
the down torn
off Uptown by the icy wind the wing the Sixth
Downtown the lovely
Downtown
turquoise.

   IV
Sucking
slowly earnestly
sucking cease-
lessly sucking without

ever tiring with all one's
soul sucking just
sucking
all sucked all
sucked close nearer
and nearer
sucked and
nearer and nearer
in and sucked
full and
fuller and fuller
sucked sucked
deeper inside
and deeper inside always
deeper inside sucked and
deeper and deeper
inside and sucked
out and always
more and more sucked out all
sucked out empty
sucked down to the dregs.


V

Hides hanging
from the walls
hides peeled
off stripped
off hides
everywhere down from
all the walls
hanging hides of
blood and flesh of bones

freed tidy
rinsed hides
on nails on clean
washed heads
of nails hides
hanging down
from the walls
the nails cleansed and scrubbed
of all the filth
from the shining heads of the nails
the hanging hides
neatly distributed across
the painfully washed
walls.

VI

If you'd only remained
back in the line and hadn't
pressed forward toward
the front they'd have
soon enough pushed you
down to stairs' lowest step they'd
have soon enough pushed
you up the stairs step
by step they'd have
soon enough held you fast they'd
have soon enough no
longer held you back no
longer let you back down
they'd

# ESCORIAL

I

Into the halls
into the rooms through all
the passages ech-
o of your steps inside
innermost the cell
the gridiron
odor of burned
flesh
and then back through the halls
the rooms through all
the passages ech-
o of your steps out
into the air the distance
tiny butterflies and white
over the bushes.

II

Or down below through the
cellars and through the
tombs the damp
cowls in shreds
falling into threads particles
colorless and musty
smelling and in the cowls
squeaking mice and ahead
at the end the chests with heavy
lids sunk
in the rubble yet in the fearful
light the steps winding and above

the distance anew
tiny butterflies and white
over the bushes.

### III

Or from tower to tower from one
gable to another the ringing
of the bells as if the judge
appeared in the heavens and not
a single cloud the white
rabbits and far
from being afraid at the foot
of the shaking cupola
munching away and in their eyes
curiosity flashing they're
destined for the evening meal.

The tigers hunt in the graben.
The stars rattle through your eye.
The tigers hunt in packs.
The tigers sniff around nights
for the stars in the graben,
which clatter to the ground
through your sleepless open eye.

If only the snow lay
far and wide on the paths by now,
if only the chickens, shrieking
scratched the corn out of the icy
tracks of the sleds,
you'd whisk easily
over the meadows, swiftly
glide down the hardened
slopes and out
across the Nile and effortlessly
reach the sphinx readied for
white feasts and Cheop's severe
pyramid still rimed.

## LABYRINTH

You pull the thread
off the roll, which is fastened
to the door, and pull it around
the mirrors and mirror-corners so that
if it weren't of nylon
it would tear.
But pulling you even harder,
inexorably, is the image
of the Minotaur, which
inside the mirrors
and the mirror-corners, hidden
in the high-flown
shrubs, blinks and yawns.

Above the flood,
the pyramid drowned. The dog
ran across the road. The flood
oozes away. Only
scarabaeus shakes its Nile-sleep
off, crawls over the dead
dog at the foot of the pyramid
covered by mold. The flood
oozes away. Only scarabaeus.

# THE THRONE

Today the servant
can't find the button which sets
the lions roaring and lets them
raise up the throne. The
emperor bites his lips.
The envoy
cuts his speech short and pays homage
to the peacock instead, which draws
its tail across the gravel.

# CARDINAL

His robe rolls
when he walks in the park
almost into the sea,
which shames him violetly back to his room.

But before he can turn completely around,
the constellation captivates him, which,
mixing its colored lights, shoots
quickly up out of the mist's seam.
So quickly he'd like to ask Saint Nicholas
to delay it
if he didn't know
it flies through unchecked to Rome
at this very hour.

Instead of his robe, there's the bed of roses
spread out along the shore,
when he drinks lemonade in his little dress
and invokes the quieter images
to stay, stay.

Though there are sometimes some sailors
coming quite close in their paddleboats
to snap his picture with the peacocks
and calling out cheerfully "Guess not then,"
when he declines their cigarettes with dignity . . .

The head in the niche
smashed and
the bloody bandages.
The column of
beetles crawling along
sluggishly.
From afar, with long
pauses in between
the echo
of drops in the gutter.

Ground down
collapsed by kisses
forgotten sold and
carried off over the water cast away
melted down in a blazing city and forgotten
again and then
the one or the other
in a ditch accidentally broken
into the one
the other of a golden coat
among cockroaches under
yellowish maggots
golden the one found
golden the other thread.

The first injured.
The second the third
injured. Before the last
kills
the odor plucked
from the hot wall.
In haste.
Before the last.

The curtain rolled up
the weight of
the porphyry on the
nape of the neck on the
arc of the blade. The holes
of the eyes sucking away
and before the entrance
the sand-glass raised up.

## BUCOLIC

But the cold
water in the black
vault. And outside
glow of cicadas. Lowered
horns of bulls.

## LOCKED UP

Taken
out
cut
out
torn
out of your
chest and carried
far far away
from its root bleeding
locked up
in the capsule of silver
locked up
and immured
in the column

locked up
your heart

*And Always Go On*  IV

# LISTENING

Listening to
the lyre
a loving soul plays in distant
gardens or a lonely
man listening to
the silhouette of our earth
listening to the moon
to the stranger among us humans
listening to the night
over mountain
heights and full of
stars sad and splendid
and listening and listening.

The sand's hot, and the pearls
scorch the yellow
glove: early today
it was pushing the pram
beyond the Syrte. Now it roots
around and finds and burns, yellow
glove, digs
beyond the Syrte,
finds pearls, burns up.

# ESCAPE

The gulf
down below turned to lead,
and higher
overhead the wild
plants are thrown together.
Higher and thicker. Soon
they'll keep you forever, so that you
won't see the gulf down below
anymore und nevermore
hear the deadly, quiet
song of the sailors.

You crouch down on the shore road, chew
the bitter leaf when the white
umbrellas draw by with their cries and
shrieks. You won't see,
won't hear
until the seal on the wave
jumps over the escarpment at your neck.
Then you forget to chew, then you run,
you're confused, crush the white
umbrellas underfoot. The wave, the cries,
the shrieking drain away. Astonished,
the seal snuffles around in the middle
of the empty shore road.

## BELOW

Below
right at the bottom of the fountain suddenly
open expanse. Sails
next to the swans. But
up through the cracks
fumes of blood.

The storms aren't able to
move the island-raft. The birds
freeze above the animals,
which have come out of the forests
beyond the desert
and thunderstruck go along
the horizon. The wind
presses them into packs.
Until in December
the birds plunge into the sea.
On New Year's Eve it washes
them into the hollows,
which our feet scraped
in summer.
Lost souls will
find the frozen birds on New Year's Day
and take them as gifts and stick
them into their tattered coats.

Seven days, sea, you're sleeping before the
new storms shake you awake, before they
chase away the kingfisher's mate,
which flies back and forth
through your dreams. Perhaps
she spots the cliff where I'm chewing
the bitter leaf soft. The storms
quicken, they drag
the kingfisher's mate into the foam, devour
the cliff. After
seven days, my sleeping one, white
and shaken awake, you forget your dreams.

## BIRD

The wave
draws the gravel into the distance and terrifies
the bird, which
fears the foam; because it
laps up insatiably, saltily. And the bird
puts on its claws and turns
out into the distance, stretches
its wings with the combs of waves.
Fish jump. Rarely
does the bird drop down on them. Mostly
it hovers, tumbles
dreamless and doesn't recall
a single one of these coasts, which
titter and tingle.

# WITHOUT

Without the processions the waves
flooding into the
fortified harbor with combs
broken and white
rising and sinking without
the memory and without the wasting longing
this web of dreams of words
without the image
no eye has seen severely
guarded in the desert: how to go on
then and on and always
go on
and always?

## WOOD

Wood under water
phosphorescent, it won't
break out
in fire. The flood
persists and keeps it covered. The ship
travels fast, and I can't
cast my anchor
as a pivot, pull
the wood up to me.

Then it'd break right
out into fire, burn
the ship up. It's casting its gray
veil over the sky now. I'm screaming
for low tide. The moon's
been taken away, the flood
persists, people are
dancing in the dark relentlessly,
drunk on the deck. My anchor
misses and can't attach as a pivot
to the wood, phosphor
shines under the water.

Down with the black wreaths
into the water. Flashes
from the impact. And then in the fog
farther toward the north.

Down and away from this
hanging root too. How soft
the wing how downy
over the woods. The waters
far below frozen
in silver. Reliquaries
of childhood.
Undeadly.

Down with the wreaths
into the drowned tunnel.
New
roots in the dark.
Neither summer nor winter.

One after the
other drawn
out and stacked
up under the
sail the tips
dried in the quiet
wind the bleeding
stilled beforehand.

The city of the dead on the cliff.
The sudden
sword of the lighthouse.
But down in the darkness the soft
surf. Soft
the cicadas.

Out there far out there
the wreck the
oily pool. Finally the storm
brings back the black
cadavers the racked
birds that died
far far out there
racked by pain.

## IN THE END

And in the end
the walls give way on both
sides the sea
blazing and still and
no edge nowhere not anywhere unless
the streak that divides the sky
divides the mists
blindly
from the giant
silvery disk.

Born in Wisconsin, STUART FRIEBERT spent an undergraduate year in Germany as one of the first U.S. exchange students after World War II (1949-50), after which he finished a Ph.D. (1957) at the University of Wisconsin at Madison in German Language & Literature. He began teaching at Mt. Holyoke College, subsequently at Harvard University, until settling at Oberlin College in 1961, where he continued teaching German until, in the mid-1970s, with help from colleagues, he founded Oberlin's Creative Writing Program, which he directed until retiring. Along the way, with colleagues, he co-founded *Field Magazine,* later the *Field Translation Series* and Oberlin College Press.

Among the fourteen books of poems he's published, *Funeral Pie* co-won the Four Way Book Award in 1997; and *Floating Heart* (Pinyon Publishing) won the Ohioana 2015 Poetry Award. In addition, he's published ten volumes of translations—most recently *Puppets in the Wind: Selected Poems of Karl Krolow* (Bitter Oleander Press, 2014) and *Be Quiet: Selected and Selected Poems by Kuno Raeber* (Tiger Bark Press, 2015). He has also published a number of stories and memoir-pieces, collected in a volume entitled *The Language of the Enemy,* published by Black Mountain Press in 2015.

CHRISTIANE WYRWA studied German and English Literature at Göttingen, Durham GB and Berlin where she took a Ph.D. in 1981. With her husband Matthias Klein, she edited Kuno Raeber's *Collected Works* in seven volumes from 2002 to 2010.